The Adventures of Sam the Strong

Written by Travis Woronowicz

Illustrations by Jashton Gieser

ISBN: 979-8-9864589-1-5 (Paperback)
ISBN: 979-8-9864589-2-2 (eBook)

THE ADVENTURES OF
SAM THE STRONG

There once was a boy named Sam. Sam was 8 years old and really, really, *really* loved space! In fact, he loved space so much that he wanted to be the first boy to live on Mars for a whole week.

That summer, Sam and his Dad built a spaceship that would take Sam to Mars. The ship was bright blue with a silver dome hatch. Inside the ship, there were many buttons for Sam to push, along with the captain's seat and a place for Sam to sleep when he got to Mars.

Dad said most ships took 6 months to get to Mars. But not Sam's ship! Sam's ship was *so fast* that it would get him to Mars in 30 minutes!

Dad suggested that Sam should give his ship a *really cool* name. Sam thought for a moment and came up with the name Space Safari 1.

SPACE
SAFARI
1
JOHN CARTER
CALVIN & HOBBES
SPACEMAN SPIFF

Sam packed up everything he needed for his trip: a few sets of clothes, his favorite snacks (granola bars, apple slices, and grapes), and his stuffed cat named Kitty. Sam thought he had all he needed, but his mom added a few more clothes and snacks when he wasn't looking.

Sam put on his special space suit and helmet. His suit was bright white with black suspenders and a Mars patch on the left arm.

As Sam was flexing his muscles and admiring his suit and helmet in the mirror, Dad walked in.

"Don't forget this," Dad said as he handed him a golden badge that said 'Sam the Strong.' "You are Sam the Strong! Don't ever forget that, son! You'll need to remember that when challenges come up. Love you, bud."

ARS
SOLAR SYSTEM
SAM
the
STRONG
NINJA
POWER

"I love you too, Dad." Sam gave Dad a hug and pinned the new badge on his suit. He really was 'Sam the Strong'!

"We're so proud of you, son," Mom said. "Have a great trip, honey. Can we pray?"

Mom grabbed Sam's hand and prayed, "Father, thank you for our son, his love for space, and the trip he's about to take. Help him remember that *You* are his strength; go with him in this, keep him safe, and bring him back safely to us. In Jesus' name we pray, amen!"

Sam hugged his little sister, kissed his mom goodbye, and pounded Dad's fist. Sam the Strong was ready for his first adventure to Mars!

Sam climbed aboard his ship and buckled himself and Kitty in. Dad walked over with a clipboard in his hand. Sam was ready to flip some switches and take off!

"Launch control, we are go for launch," Dad said to Mom. Mom gave him a thumbs-up.

"I love you!" she shouted over the whirring engines.

"Love you too," Sam said as he pulled down the hatch and clicked it into place.

"Countdown to launch," Dad said. "10, 9, 8, 7, 6, 5, 4, 3, 2, 1, blastoff!"

At that, a bright orange fire came out of the back of Sam's ship, and Sam blasted into the sky and out of their sight.

RED ROVER
1952

Sam screamed with delight as his ship flew faster than any roller coaster he had ever been on before! "Woo-hoooooooo!"

As Sam blasted off, his little sister was very happy to see him go. She had all the toys to herself now! So long, Sam!

Sam's ship tore through the clouds with ease, and in moments, the sky in front of him changed from bright blue to pitch black (with little pinpricks of light shining through).

Sam had never seen stars so beautiful before! "Look at all these stars, Kitty! I can't believe we're doing this! Mars, get ready for the adventures of Sam the Strong! Here we come!"

As Sam's ship zoomed through the blackness of space, he noticed the rusty red planet of Mars getting bigger in his window. It was first the size of a marble, then the size of a kickball, and then the red floor of Mars was now all Sam could see.

Sam grabbed the joystick and started the landing sequence. He started moving the joystick left and then right, and when he thought his ship was in the correct position to land, he pressed the bright red landing button.

The fire in the back of his ship went out, and for the next few seconds, Sam felt the way you feel when you first zoom down the hill of a huge roller coaster. After a few more seconds, his ship finally crashed to the ground with a crunch and a thud.

Sam shook off the hard landing and slowly opened the hatch. His ship was smoking all over, and pieces of his ship were covering the ground as far as his eyes could see. Even though it would take a while to fix, Sam didn't care. He was on Mars!

As he climbed down the ladder, Kitty firmly in hand, Sam jumped onto the dusty planet with both feet. "That's one small step for Kitty and one giant leap for Sam the Strong!"

Sam kneeled to the ground, scooped up some reddish-brown dirt in his hands, and thanked God for getting him there safely. With his finger, he spelled 'Sam the Strong was here' in the dirt, put a few Mars rocks in his pocket, and started looking around.

Everything was still and quiet until he heard a scraping noise in the distance. Sam hid behind the biggest rock he could find and listened as a shiny metallic rover rolled in his direction. The rover stopped in front of the rock he was hiding behind, and a laser beam started to scan the area for life.

"Human boy recognized," Rover said. "Identify yourself immediately."

Knowing his cover was blown, Sam stepped out from behind the rock. "I am Sam the Strong. I come from Earth. I'm staying here for a week. And what are you doing here, Rover?"

"I was sent here to look for life. You are not the first life to be found here..."

"Wait...are you saying there are *other* life-forms here?"

"Yes, human boy."

"Where are they?" Sam asked excitedly. "Can I see them?"

"I will take you to them now. Prepare to follow."

As Rover turned around and rolled away from their location, Sam had to remind himself to follow its lead (instead of jumping ahead of it). That was hard for Sam as he liked to be the leader. But he remembered that the best leaders were followers first, so he followed the best he could.

After a few minutes of walking behind Rover, they stopped beside a bunch of deep-looking holes in the ground. Sam crouched down and saw a small creature peeking out from one of the holes.

Sam made a clicking noise, and much to his surprise, the creature came out cautiously. It looked like a light green meerkat with dark green hands and feet and bright orange eyes.

Sam reached into his pocket, grabbed out some of his apple slices, and offered them to the creature. It ate the slices happily, and from that point on, it would be Sam's first official pet on Mars.

Sam named the creature 'Stinky Bobo' (a name that made him laugh every time he said it).

"Human boy, there are other creatures to be seen. Follow me."

Rover rolled away from the hole in the rocks and brought Sam to what looked like a pond at some point. The ground was dry and cracked, and there were rocks everywhere.

"Look behind that rock," Rover said. As Sam slowly peered behind the rock, he found an animal that looked like a turtle. It had a thick blue shell and scaly skin that was a lima bean green. Unlike Stinky Bobo, the turtle wasn't afraid of Sam.

"I think I will call you Leonardo because you remind me of one of my favorite cartoons back home!"

Before Sam could turn around, there was a bright red bird-like creature that swooped down and landed on his arm! The creature had a yellow mohawk that started on its head and went down its entire back.

"Look at this bird!" Sam exclaimed.

"Look at this bird!" it answered back to him!

"You can talk?" Sam said, amazed.

"You can talk," repeated the bird again.

"This is great! I think I will call you Mohawk, for obvious reasons."

Sam was elated to now have three creature friends on Mars, besides Kitty and Rover. He asked Rover if there were more creatures but wasn't expecting what Rover said next.

"Yes, human boy, there are more creatures. They live in Cave City, but they are in trouble. Should I initiate the travel sequence to take you to them now?"

Sam looked at his new friends, and knew he had to do something. He nodded to Rover, and Sam, Kitty, Stinky Bobo, Leonardo, and Mohawk all followed Rover to the City.

It seemed as though Rover was rolling in front of them for hours. But soon the entrance to the cave loomed in the distance. "Use caution, human boy, as we enter the cave. It will be dark at first but will then open up into a vast city. Prepare to enter."

Rover went in ahead of them and shined a light so they could see. Sam walked into the cave behind Rover, and his friends followed cautiously after him.

Instead of being cold and damp, this cave was dark and dusty. Sam kept a watch on his steps, and after a few minutes, he saw the clearing that opened into the massive city.

The city was bigger than Sam imagined. There were giant rock structures with openings for windows and doors chiseled into them. Sam looked from left to right and noticed many colorful dinosaur-looking creatures scurrying in every direction.

"Rover, you said there were creatures in trouble here. Are these the creatures you were talking about?"

"Yes, human boy, these are the creatures I told you about. This is their city, they built it, but an enemy found it and wants it for himself. Every day he comes here and harasses them. He told them that he will not stop until they surrender their city to him."

"Enemy, what enemy?" Sam asked, not wanting to be around for that. But before Rover could answer, Sam knew he was about to find out. He heard the little dinosaur creatures screaming and running from the center square.

"I am Mogag-man, and I am here to claim this city!" the creature roared. He had the face of an ugly old dog but the body of a well-built man. He had a huge club in his hand, and he looked like he meant business.

Sam was afraid of this beast and hid just out of his view. He wanted nothing more than to get back to his ship and get home. As he thought about this, he noticed a blue dinosaur with yellow spots, hiding next to him and shaking all over.

"Hi, there. I'm Sam," Sam said, causing the blue dinosaur to jump in the air.

"Oh, hi. I didn't see you there," the animal said. "My name is Shi. This is *our* city, but that nasty Mogag-man won't leave us alone. He thinks he can just come in here and take this city as his own because we're too weak to stop him!"

Just then, Shi noticed the golden badge on Sam's suit that said 'Sam the Strong.'

"Do you think *you* could help us?"

"Geez, I don't know," Sam said. "I'm just as scared of Mogag-man as you guys are. Maybe I'm not really Sam the Strong after all."

"But your badge *says* 'Sam the Strong,'" insisted Shi. "Who gave that to you?"

Sam looked down at his golden badge. "My Dad gave it to me. He told me to not forget and that I'd need to remember it when challenges came up. My Mom prayed that I would be strong, too, and that God would be my strength. I don't feel very strong, though."

The little blue dinosaur looked Sam in the eyes. He had stopped shaking and looked stronger than before.

"It sounds like your Mom and Dad love you and believe God can help you *be* Sam the Strong. Can you trust them, Sam? We can't beat Mogag-man on our own, but perhaps God can make us all strong and courageous to beat him together!"

Sam looked at the little blue dinosaur and then looked at Kitty, Rover, Stinky Bobo, Leonardo, and Mohawk. Perhaps God *would* help them find a way to beat Mogag-man with *His* strength and courage flowing through them. Sam crouched down in the dirt, looked his friends in the eyes, and started to talk through a strategy of how to take down the big, mean Mogag-man.

As Mogag-man circled the center square, shouting all sorts of threats to the dinosaur creatures, Sam stepped up and shouted up to him, "You'll have to go through me first! I am Sam the Strong!"

Mogag-man turned around, saw Sam standing there, and laughed a deep, nasty belly laugh.

"Are you kidding me? You think *you* can beat me? Forget it!" Mogag-man roared.

"Not just me, but *us*, and not just us, but *God through us*! Leave my friends alone once and for all!"

At that, Stinky Bobo used Sam's golden badge to reflect Rover's light into Mogag-man's eyes. Blinded by the light, he stumbled backward, but he didn't see Leonardo behind him, hiding in his shell like a big rock. Tripping over Leonardo, Mogag-Man fell backward with a thud. Mohawk then flew overhead and dropped a boulder on his head. Stunned by the boulder, a group of red, orange, purple, blue, black, green, and yellow dinosaurs ran toward him with ropes in their tiny hands. They tied him up as quickly as they could, and with *God's help* that day, they had defeated Mogag-man once and for all!

With all the creatures standing over Mogag-man victoriously, Shi thanked Sam for believing that God could make him 'Sam the Strong.'

Although his fear was *really* loud that day, Sam was glad he didn't listen to his fear. That wouldn't have helped him or his friends.

Instead, Sam was glad that he faced this challenge with courage, that he was able to help his friends, and that he was becoming Sam the Strong more and more.

Sam and his friends made it back to his ship. He forgot that it was broken into a bunch of different pieces and needed fixing.

"Rover, is this something I can fix?" Sam asked as Rover scanned the damage.

"No, you cannot fix it on your own. But with the help of your new friends, we should be able to have you out of here by the end of the week."

Sam smiled as Rover projected the blueprints on the rocks. And with the help of his new friends, Sam the Strong was able to fix his ship and make it home by the end of the week.

SPACE SAFARI 2

When he got home, his Mom, Dad, and sister ran out to meet him.

"Hi, honey, how was your trip?"

"It was awesome, Mom. I can't wait to go back. But until I do, I have a question." At this, the little blue dinosaur poked his head out from Sam's backpack, and smiled.

Mom and Dad gasped as Sam puffed out his chest and strongly asked if he could keep him. They rolled their eyes, laughed, and hugged their space-traveling son who really was growing into his new name.

Have I not commanded you? Be strong and courageous.
Do not be frightened, and do not be dismayed,
for the Lord your God is with you wherever you go.
(Joshua 1:9)

I just wanted to express my deepest gratitude to all of you who financially supported the publishing of this book through GoFundMe:

1. Patty Pulver
2. Sharon Harding and Brian Gilling
3. The Bestvina Family
4. Susan Strickland
5. Peter and Rachel Johnson
6. Susan and Raiden Westad
7. Tim and Nancy Egan
8. Paul and Katie Alvarez
9. Tom and Elena Marcelle
10. Adam and Lindsay Porto
11. Perry and Susan Jones
12. Amanda Caldwell
13. Nick and Grace Gervais
14. Rachel Gehr
15. Matt Lawrence
16. Uncle Andy and Aunt Tara
17. Edward Woronowicz
18. Jesse Gardner
19. Rick and Betsy D'Errico
20. John Messina
21. Dirk and Jennifer Gieser
22. Chris Jones
23. David Ewert
24. Seth Heydinger
25. Dave and Cody Woronowicz
26. David Layton
27. Nathaniel Martin
28. David Harding
29. Samuel and Chelsea Foster
30. Matthew and Karen Hogan
31. Dan and Heather Kissling
32. William VanEvra
33. Caryl and Rosalind Thompson
34. Kenrick Permaul
35. Darius and Karen Kirstein
36. + All of you who wanted to remain anonymous!

If the message of *The Adventures of Sam the Strong* resonated with you, here are **three ways** you can bless your children practically:

1. Think through some important character traits found in the Scriptures: being strong, kind, compassionate, honest, joyful, loving, loyal, humble, patient, peaceful, good, faithful, gentle, etc. Pick one of these characteristics and start using it after your child's name FOR A WHOLE YEAR. Then pick a new characteristic the following year, and try it again!

2. In his book *The 5 Love Languages*, Gary Chapman suggests that we receive love in one of the following five ways: physical touch, words of affirmation, quality time, gifts, or acts of service. Consider the ways your children receive love the best and find ways to participate in those things (the way they like doing them).

3. Pray biblical prayers over your kids. Pray they would come to know Jesus as their Savior and Lord (Romans 3:23, 6:23, 5:8, Ephesians 2:8-9, John 14:6, John 3:16), that they would learn to hear His voice and follow Him (John 10:27, Matthew 4:19), and that God would make it real to their hearts about how He sees them (Genesis 32:24-30, Numbers 6:24-26, Luke 3:21-22).

Or if you found yourself longing for a blessing from your Heavenly Father, but don't know how to access that, consider emailing me at samthestrongbook@gmail.com or checking out the Luke 10 Community (https://LK10.com). I'd love to talk with you more about this!

About the Author

Travis Woronowicz is a follower of Jesus who is called to know Jesus and make Him known through preaching, teaching, writing, drawing, and disciple-making. He went to school at Word of Life Bible Institute, Cairn University, and Mid-America Baptist Theological Seminary. Travis lives in New York with his wife, Rachel, and their two kids, Sam and Anna. He enjoys reading and creating stories with his kids.